WHAT LUCK

POEMS

SUZANNE O'CONNELL

GARDEN OAK PRESS
Rainbow, California
gardenoakpress.com

Garden Oak Press
1953 Huffstatler St., Suite A
Rainbow, CA 92028
760 728-2088
gardenoakpress.com
gardenoakpress@gmail.com

First published by Garden Oak Press on March 15, 2019
ISBN-13: 978-1-7323753-2-1
ISBN-10: 1-7323753-2-1

Printed in the United States of America

Thanks and Love
to this beloved branch of my family:

Tommy	*cat*
Orpheus	*cat*
Prometheus	*cat*
Annie	*dog*
Belle	*dog*
Bob	*dog*
Len	*cat*
Charlie	*dog*
Deener	*dog*
Ruby	*dog*
Hudson	*dog*

By the same author

A Prayer for Torn Stockings

"Not the harshness, but the way this world can be known by pushing against it. And feeling something pushing back."

– JACK GILBERT

CONTENTS

2: MY BODY THE BILLBOARD

WHAT LUCK

POEMS

SUZANNE O'CONNELL

GARDEN OAK PRESS

1

ONE INCH OF LAND

Chances Are

Two mothers sit in a living room.
If you look in through the window,
you might think the afternoon light
is smoke from a grey forest fire.

They sit, cocktails in hand,
pretending they're in a dark bar –
no responsibilities.
no children.
no need to watch the clock.

They sit in the living room surrounded
by chicken lamps and dented mahogany furniture.
They sink deep into the old sofa.
In the corner is a half finished science project,
glue spilled on the table, popsicle sticks and
cardboard litter the rug.

Johnny Mathis sings from the record player.
He sings about love and missed chances.
The mothers pile up their regrets
like unpaid bills.
They want someone to look at them
with stars from the skies in their eyes.

If you look through the window
as the gray smoke seeps in, you might
catch a glimpse of children
running through the front door,
arms thrown around necks of their mothers.

For a moment from that angle,
it is unclear
if the mothers are being
loved or strangled.

My Captive

I stalked her petticoats like a caged shrimp,
noticed when she shaved her legs,
when her skirt was an inch shorter,
when she wore two different white socks,
traced the raisin-shaped scar on her knee.

A thread dangled from her hem,
a tease, a mystery that would unlock
the other side of the world.
I imagined what would happen
if I pulled it.

Would she unravel?
Become a cocoon spinning toward me?
Could I use it to tie her to the tetherball pole?
She never noticed me once.
I could wrap that thread around my finger –
a reminder never to forgive her.

Sepia Tones

Even when pushing through mountains
with a rusty drill bit,
some children, like dogs,
don't complain.

"I pay the bills around here," he said.
I watched his breath go in and out.
His breath vibrated in sepia tones.
I thought about his death so many hours.

"I'll give you something to cry about," he said
as a splinter entered my heart.
His thick fingers tapped the adding machine
and his anger bumped into the furniture.

I hid behind the couch,
my membranes silent, my eyes closed,
concealed from the words that
sizzled around me like bullets.

I thought about his death so many hours.
Now that he's finally gone,
I want him back.
I want to complain to his face,
like a fierce dog on a chain.

Listening to Errol Garner

Your hands
served on different committees.
The left
was as smooth as your brilliantined hair.
The right,
mischievous,
tickled one note, paused,
then slipped down a glass stairway.

Next,
a feint,
a repeat,
a kiss at the train station.
Oh Errol,
that bowlegged swagger of yours,
while your left hand
marked the steps.

Your touch was gentle.
You freed a melody
trapped under silk.
You skipped,
bumped,
stumbled
my beating heart.

And your stride! Baby, that stride.

Sometimes There's Nothing Better
than a Car Chase on TV

Part of me hoped the driver would get away.
I admired his determination.
He kept going even though
the spike strip popped all his tires.
I know what it's like to need to escape.

His black car sped
through the glittering L.A. streets,
metal rims on asphalt
blowing a trail of sparks behind him
into the darkness.

It reminded me of the shoes
I bought for my first job.
Black kitten heels, my only shoes,
except for white sneakers.
I wore those black shoes to work every day
where I was granted a Top Secret clearance.
I printed classified documents
on a Xerox machine bigger than a car.
My neighbors were interviewed by an FBI agent
who asked if the 18-year-old girl
who resided at 1040 Euclid Street
could be trusted with the security of the nation.

I learned about other classified information too,
like my boss' affair with our big boss.
Both were married.
Both ordered me to make excuses
for their long lunches,
for their loud arguments.

I Xeroxed and lied.
I wore out my shoes.
I lost the rubber heel tips first.
Then the wooden stumps splintered.
Then nails emerged, snagging carpet
and scraping pavement.

The lies felt too familiar.
Just like the lies in my family.
I quit my job.
I packed my few belongings,
my Top Secret name badge,
my comb,
my address book.
my packets of Tomato Cup 'O Soup.
I stomped out the door on my nails,
listening as they scraped the sidewalk.
As I walked away,
a trail of sparks blew behind me
into the darkness.

Taking Measures

Last night I baked her in a crust,
shiny like challah.
Vents were cut
for steam and for her breathing.

Her eye spied me
through a vent. She blinked,
moved. She was alive.
Safe.

As a child I carried pussy willows
in my pocket, stroked their fur.
They never roamed. Dolls
were confined to my orphanage.

I am a stranger here.
Sooner or later, your beautifuls
will leave.
Measures must be taken.

Tie them down.
Lock your doors.
Or bake them in a pie.

I Ignored All Advice

Cats slept in my cradle.
Hummingbirds flew round my eyes.
I swam directly after a meal,
ate a raw egg,
went into the cellar after a sound,
did not wear a scarf,
and mixed milk with meat.

Death is all fancy language
shaped by one's luck.
I learned to identify falderol.
I laughed in death's face.
Hairs on my head were
wild weeds that insisted on living,
wheat and roots,
plumb lines into my ancestry.

In the cold garden of time,
I played without a jacket,
put my hands in the dirt,
talked to strangers,
and petted chickens.
No knocking knees for me.
No advice heeded.

And when, many years hence,
the bony arm finally grasps me
by the button,
pulls me to the black cavern,
dresses me in the wrapping cloth,

the advice givers can say,
There, I told you so.

Gentle Bones

I.

Darkness is upon us all.
The old tree kneels
like always
to sip from the water.

Poison pen letters
were returned
for insufficient postage.
Girls wear safety pins
and march in the street.

The house is dark.
The dachshund-shaped lamp,
is steadfast,
sitting in its halo of light.

II.

Darkness is upon us.
Search for the tiny miracles
close enough to touch.
Your ears for example,
those workaday wings.

Hello gentle bones,
hello flexible trumpets
made for listening.
You can touch the silken skin,
move them as in flight.
Their perfect rims
are crimped like pies
for our tarnished Thanksgiving.

The Night Grandma Died
I Dreamed I Robbed a Bank

The last time I saw grandma,
she was in the Arbor View Nursing Home.
There was no arbor, no view.
Grandma complained that her roommate
had sex in her hospital bed every night.
When I asked her if she needed anything,
she said a different roommate.
And, she added,
black fishnet stockings
and two cans of Schlitz.

The night grandma died,
I dreamed I robbed a bank.
There was a bee in the getaway car.
I steered with one hand,
swatted at the bee with the other.
I drove faster, downhill.
I could hear sirens.
I cranked the window down
to let the bee escape.
Wind opened my money bag.
Cash flew like a green snowstorm in the car.
The sirens got louder.
Then I woke up.

When I was six,
grandma and I sat in rocking chairs on her porch,
a bowl of mocha ice cream cold between my thighs.
I read Shakespeare to her,
I brushed her gray hair.
I threw apple peels over my shoulder
to reveal my future husband's initial.
She asked what I wanted to be when I grew up?
I said I wanted to be a bank robber,
so I could buy her
an inside bathroom
chicken not from a can
real fake teeth
and all the Schlitz she wanted.

Fire in My Neighborhood

They said jump to the black places.
So we hopscotched through what
was once our neighborhood.
Steam rose from the broken concrete
as we surfed through walls of fire.
Deer passed us, going
the opposite direction.
And the heat. I had no earthly idea.
The heat created a new natural element
that combined fire and air.
I named it Chinese Sky Lantern.
Because as we got hotter,
and there were no more black places,
we became bubbles.
We filled ourselves with light that night,
floated over sticks of trees,
melted cars,
footprints of houses.
We became Chinese Sky Lanterns
and we floated away.

Where Do Angels Fly?

As I walked home,
a puff of smoke blew out of the bush.
"Where can I get a donut?" a man's voice yelled.
I carried heavy market bags. It was late.
There was a rustling in the bushes.
I noticed a cigarette's glow through
the leaves.
I could smell acrid smoke.

His voice was like scissors in an artery.
Like a child's first violin lesson.
Like the bite of a wild hyena.

Oh! The angels among us! Where do they fly
when they tire of this silvered plain?
Sometimes the tops of trees are like
perfume bottles that release a piney fragrance,
a handsoap for God's dirt.

I was supposed to cook for Thanksgiving.
I've got to remember to check the calendar.
I've got to learn to read a recipe.
I've got to learn to cook.

Why a donut?" I asked.
"Why not a main course, plus three sides and pie?
Or warm clothes?
Or an apartment?

"Because I'm a Scorpio," he answered.
"My forecast today says I need to lower my expectations."

My heavy frozen turkey
bled in the paper bag
as I walked toward home.

A Child's Prayer

Link the fingers,
a beginner's chain.
Use your two hands,
two hands,
your two hands.

Flatten your palms,
a simple thing.
Press your two palms,
two palms,
your two palms.

Lift the pointers.
Skyward sisters,
up they go.
Two pointers,
lift your pointers.

Prayers can be said anywhere.
Knees or no knees.
The church,
the steeple.
Open wide
and let in the people.

Let in the people.
Your people.
All of them.
All of them.
Please let them in.
Amen.

Asphalt

Your arms waved for help.
The policeman bent down, hand on gun.
"No!" you shouted.
He fired.
The sound, an exploding beehive.
I looked at your fragile skull, resting
on the sharp leaves of fall.
Your eyelashes blinked.

Helicopters circled, sirens came.
Your blood kept pooling.
It was the color of mine.
I saw the snow catch in your curly hair.

You had something in your hand,
a Black Cow caramel bar.
"It Lasts All Day," the wrapper said.

Connie and Dean

I lifted the screen off the sliding door.
Even the dog didn't hear me.
It smelled like scrambled eggs
inside her condo.
First I got rid of the dog.
Then her friend Sue.

Lying on the closet floor,
Connie's eyes looked dreamy,
two stained glass windows at sundown.
Her body, crunched like a possum,
on the side of a dark road.
Her face was an innocent clock
going backwards.
"Dean, it's over," her last letter said.

Most days I just got by.
She wouldn't pick up my calls.
She wouldn't see me.

I told her I loved her.
I put a pillow under her head.
I combed her hair, lay down
next to that gorgeous body,
put my arm around her waist.

She was my only language.
Now on the closet floor,
she had nothing further to say.

The Science Lesson

Last night, my grandson explained
that gravitational waves exist,
an extra ocean up above.
I didn't understand him.

As he spoke, I pictured
my ankles in the ocean,
waves rippling around them
like waves might flow
around black holes.

Our transparent nature
is but a skinny voice,
a wisp of wire that connects us
to the universe.

My grandson,
my teacher,
my miracle,
I don't understand him either.

He pastes his used contact lenses
to the bedroom wall,
creating a new universe,
an ocean of tiny sparkling mirrors.

Underneath

Under the flesh of Wilshire Blvd,
while digging the new subway,
they found an ice age mammoth skull.
Centuries later, it waits,
eyes like empty fishbowls,
majestic tusks
raised skyward.

My tires rolled over that very spot,
bruised the soil, didn't know
that bones underneath flinched.
Seasons changed.
Thoughtless leaves mulched the asphalt.
Summer's children rode bikes,
war protesters marched with placards,
homeless people pushed carts,
food trucks selling kimchi burritos,
traveled over,
never knowing what was down there.

Under my own flesh,
a brain artery could pop.
A bunch of bad cells could copulate.
There could be chemo and other nasty stuff.
Or, I could be broadsided during a green light.
A crazy dictator could push the red button.
There could be a tax audit, the poorhouse maybe.
Or my husband could realize he's attracted to men.
I ask you. How do we go on?
With all the danger lurking underneath?

The Sleeping Bag

The girl, wearing her crisp flesh and new shoes,
walked past what looked like a discarded sleeping bag.
Then she noticed feet sticking out, soiled shoes,
knees to chest, dirty pants, hoodie over face.
A small bundle of human,
lying in the middle of the sidewalk.

The girl could have put down her leather purse,
opened the silver clasp,
reached for her phone,
called for help.
But she didn't want to interfere,
didn't want to touch the soiled discard.
What if they told her to do CPR?
The breathing kind over the mouth?
After all, the bundle made its own choices,
right?

The girl walked to her car,
sat on the plush seats,
smelled the lavender air freshener
that hung from her mirror.
She turned the air conditioning to high,
drove away listening to Springsteen
sing something about gates of hardened steel
surrounding the mansion on the hill.

The Wrong Name

Her mother named her Suzanne.
Her mother hoped that all the Frenchness
of the name
would be conferred upon the girl.
Suzanne was instructed to tell others
she was French,
not to mention her Irish grandmother
who wove fabric in a factory.

The gamine haircut,
like Leslie Caron, looked ungainly
upon Suzanne's cheeky Irish face.
She demonstrated no
aptitude for language,
especially Francais.

Suzanne had no taste for shallots
or tricky bernaise sauce.
Instead she preferred
fish and chips with vinegar.
Hats looked comical
on her large peasant head.
She was clumsy, not sophisticated.

She disappointed her mother
in a thousand ways,
but if her mother had only
named her Pegarty,
perhaps their relationship would
have stood a chance.

How I Dealt with Terrible News

I filled the sink with hot water,
squirted in detergent.
The street was dark and quiet.
I heard a car stop, the newspaper landed
on the damp lawn.
Each plate, each bowl, each spoon
baptized with a prayer.
I rubbed each one like the bottom
of a beloved baby,
patted, rinsed,
set to drip on the rack.

I poured hot water over the grounds.
The skunk smell of coffee filled the kitchen.
I prepared the mugs with milk and sugar.
Stirred slowly.
Squeezed four tangerines from our tree
into special glasses, the ones
with the glass bees.
I wiped the sticky counter clean,
prepared the tray with paper towels
mugs, glasses, and dog treats.

Oh ordinary life,
so boring,
so daily,
so predictable.
Why didn't I worship you before?

What I Know About Tradition
is Nothing

If this were a memoir, I would say
we were the Swanson TV Dinner people.
It was our only tradition.

We sat around the black and white TV set
every Friday night with our aluminum tins.
The indentations held turkey and applesauce,
or roast beef and mashed potatoes.

I wanted other traditions,
ones that reflected the skeletons of ancestors.
I wanted traditions as solid as locomotives,
flanks of iron, slowing on the downhill, then
speeding up through the small towns of my life.

If a Tree Falls

Multicolored lichen
grow up the legs of night.
My backpack is filled
with lint and stale biscuits.

Three times I call out,
Night, This Is Your Last Chance!
But there is no answer.

There is always a flame to walk toward.
There is always a hammer.
There is always the wind.

In dreams, I walk on a path
that sparkles in the moonlight.
In dreams my backpack is a cage of light.
In dreams, I call out to the night,
and it answers.

The Snow Globe

While I'm in bed reading,
you are in the hospital up north
lying on a steel table.

As I turn the pages of Science Times,
electrodes are being pasted to your temples.
They will zap your brain,
removing layer by layer
the contaminated documents,
until (hopefully)
they can locate the pristine original.

I imagine your brain as a snow globe.
During your treatment,
the snow falls up, down, and sideways.
The little girl on the path turns blue.
Her mouth hangs open.
The sky is filled with lightening bolts,
and the fur on the dog stands on end.

If the treatment works, maybe
the snow will fall softly again on the little house.
There will be no thunder or lightening.
And the little dog will scamper up the path
to the open front door where you will smile,
as the dog jumps into your arms.

Martyrs

When I was a boggy girl,
trapped in the pew,
lace hankie on my head,
and the organ vibrated my mystic lips,
I read in the holy book about
tortured martyrs.

Later, I danced through the black-eyed susans
while parrots flew over the palms.
I thought of the martyr's severed limbs
stacked like wooden clubs at the bowling alley
round the corner, where a man
crouched in the dark, lined up the pins.

The whole of the moon
I could salt like a cracker and eat.
The whole of my bed
I could sleep exquisite.
But loud words and banging pans
flew like broken airplanes from the kitchen
and the frozen mouse stayed frozen,
an icebaby, in the drainpipe.

No longer the boggy girl,
my bones ache from the crouching.
Gray thieves weave my hair.
When I try to capture sleep,
renegade marbles of thought
roll round my mind.
In my shroud, I will head for
the cold grassy room,
lace hankie over my face.
No parrots will fly there and no moon.

We are all born martyrs.

My Downstairs Neighbors

How can they choose to live like that?
So many people crammed into every room.
Babies crying. Toilets flushing day and night.
Snores rise in the darkness.
I picture them lined up like enchiladas in a pan.

I never speak to them.
They don't speak English.
I walk up my stairs and look straight ahead.
They don't even have a car.
How do they get around?

Yet sometimes during the day,
when I'm by myself studying,
or trying to write a paper,
I hear them laughing, big hearty laughs
like a bowl of punch
being passed around.
And sometimes in the evening
I can smell the onions
and meat cooking on their stove.
I lick my lips.

Their clothes are worn.
The women have long black hair
and they never go to the beauty salon.
They aren't thin either, probably because
of all those babies they have.
One woman wears the same grey sweater
every single day.

Yet one night when I came home,
I looked in their window as I walked up the stairs.
It must have been her birthday,
there was a cake, candles were lit.
A group of them were gathered around the table.
She was smiling, wearing the same old grey sweater.
She had her arms around her husband's neck.
She was looking into his eyes, kissing him.

It was then I stopped asking myself
how they can live like that.

Armaments

Usually my moat protects.
Armaments and slings
line my hillsides.
Projectiles and clay cannon balls,
metal guns anchored into rock.
Rope traps with spikes upward
greet the intruder.

My mother, the enemy,
was walled off from me by jungle tactics,
sophisticated weaponry,
dirty fighting,
and distance.

That is until yesterday.
A memory snuck through.
Like a Chinese box with magic openers,
one last slider, then a button,
Boing! I was open.
Unguarded.
Feelings of tenderness filled me.

When she made my lunch,
there would be two hardboiled eggs.
She would take waxed paper,
sprinkle salt and pepper,
fold it stamp size and include
the little envelope with the eggs.
She didn't have to go to that trouble.
The memory of that tiny parcel
cracked open
the hardboiled egg of me.

How to Make Candy

Skip the hardball stage.
Warm your machete.
Climb the tree for a coconut.
You, night swimmer, won't find it difficult.

Perform the cocoanut crust
mix with fingers until warm.
Remember, dad lied for you.
Place in a buttered munchmeal press.

Heat until the anger rises.
One, two, three, night, morning.
Heat until the undergut contracts
from the hot sides.

You will know it's done
when the inward Christian soldier says so.
You will know it's done
when you sprinkle spice on top
and know you're a girl.

Of Ghosts and Clouds

Grandma gave me a salt shaker.
She said if I sprinkled salt on the wings of a bird,
it would be mine.
I ran, I salted, I chased. They flew away
on their invisible roads.

Memories are like the sky roads
birds travel on.
Invisible or ignored,
memories surround us like ghosts and clouds.

Birds are majorettes of the wind,
paper flappers made for no purpose,
their winged dinosaur bones
commute above us.

In my birdbath, they bump butts,
gossip in ak mak voices.
God's party favors, they flit and twit.
Their hearts, the size of a kernel of rice,
beat with flurried effort.

I remember my grandmother.
My child heart, the size of a cough drop,
warmed and melted when she smiled.
She had no teeth. I didn't care.
Under her old fashioned dress,
she wore a girdle.
She never went to a beauty salon.
She drank beer,
not fancy cocktails.
No church for her, though
her gray hair was tucked round like a halo.

When I look beyond my birdbath,
I see a grown woman sitting on the bed.
She is not invisible,
not extinct.
She is learning to fly.

And So I Stood Up

And so I stood up.
It was during a thunderstorm.
The door opened.
The wind blew.
I lost time, a teenager again.
My mother walked through the door.
She didn't know anything.
She was a dish mixed all together.
Like succotash.
She had the density of a star,
not the movie kind, but celestial.
Density and destiny, the same dark matter.
All her particles were serious.
She was the dense star the family
orbited around.
Things stayed that way
until memory
outran her body.

One Inch of Land

Living in the barrens,
a child of bruised light,
I practiced folding.
That was me,
small and compact.
I couldn't say no.
I couldn't ask to roll the car window down
on a hot summer day.
I did not own the place where I stood.
Or sat, kneeled, or lay.

On my seventh birthday,
my grandfather gave me
a deed for one inch of land in Alaska.
He sent Quaker Oats box tops to Battle Creek, Michigan.
The Big Inch Land Company in Alaska made it official.
A deal was a deal.
I was a landowner.
I pictured the Yukon with loyal sled dogs and deep snow.

    I had a deed!
    I smoothed it out,
    bent the edges,
    slipped it over.
    Over and under.
    Slipped it,
    flipped it.
    Framed
    and hung it on my wall.

My inch of land,
close to the bone,
over the top,
pride upon pride.
I began to stretch out,
speak,
roll down windows,
take up space.
Who knew one inch could expand a life?

The Ant Farm

*Yoko Ono said that as a child she didn't
care about material things. She only
wanted a mother who packed her lunch box.*

For my 10th birthday I got a *Paint By Numbers Kit*
and an *Ant Farm*. There were always lots of gifts
on my birthday. And on Christmas, gifts would
spill from under the tree and cover half the room.

The canvas depicted three roses in a vase.
The paints, in capsules the size of vitamins,
were numbered. The brush was tiny and too soft
to easily stay within the tiny numbered spaces.
After one rose, different shades of pink, I gave up.

But the *Ant Farm* was a big success.
I watched the inhabitants form their tunnels
from side to side, one on top of the other.
Where were they going?
I watched them eat, sleep, and carry their dead.
But it was the tunnels that fascinated me.
The teamwork as they dug.
The sense of community.
They had a plan and they stuck to it.

Day after day, I watched the hardy little fellows
dig their tunnels to nowhere I could identify.
I watched. I remembered. I gathered inspiration
as I plotted my escape.

If You Are Lost in the Forest

Remain still.
Crouch.
Hold your breath.
Any tremor will reveal fear.
For the moment,
put a muzzle on death.

Slip off any bitterness
Put your gloves on,
loosen the clever grip
you spent years developing.
Abandon any dinner plans.
There's work to do.

Speaking of dinner,
think like a butcher,
a contortionist.
a cavity.
a defector.

To survive in the forest
put a muzzle on sorrow.
Sorrow swells when it contacts moisture.
Sorrow bloats a heart like too much salt.
Sorrow gets tangled in the wires.

Crunch the gravel on the path
to the checkpoint.
Crunch the gravel coursing
through the bloodstream.
Remember the safe word.

Stay low.
Keep walking.

Mine Are Mine

To some children,
all grandmothers are Jewish.
To others,
fathers cause earthquakes.
Eating the seed of an apple will grow
a stomach tree.
Elevators can eat people.
After all, passengers who get on
are different from the ones who get off.

Take a heart in your own two hands,
twist it like a wet rag.
The droplets that fall are yours,
as mine are mine.

When mornings are dark,
they can be called night.
Cause a ruckus.
Call the small town of your life
love.
Unlearn what others call it.
Then you will discover
what love really means.

Heaven's Fire Escape

September 11, 2001

After dust burns, where does it go?
Does it become a color?
Does it become a solid?
Does it sharpen like a box cutter?

The fire escape stretches upward,
a metal beanstalk,
passing windows of contentment,
up an impossible 86 stories.

Man, a hopeful animal,
drinks coffee on the fire escape,
watches the sun rise,
feels sunshine on his shoulders.

The red geranium
wakes in its pot on the metal step,
stretches its chlorophyll,
thinks it will be a lovely day.

The sunrise becomes
a thunder of dust.
Storms of paper scuttle,
blow in hard,
cover the geranium.
Dead things float on the coffee.
The man smells jet fuel
as a dust ruffle tucks around the fire escape.

Sacred dust.
Sacred angels.
Sacred man,
who remains steadfast in hopefulness,
despite
the taste of dust on his lips.

The Last Sandwich

"Come in and make your sister's lunch," my mother said.
The summer sun was shining and my team was up.
I was going to kick the ball next and score.

"Come in and make your sister's lunch right now,"
my mother said, louder.
"Oh fart!" I said. It was the only swear word I knew.
"What did you say?" my mother asked.

As I stomped into the kitchen, I heard
cheers rising from the rival team on the lawn.
My face felt hot and prickly.
This will be the last sandwich she ever eats, I thought.

I pulled out the Wonder Bread and the Skippy
and spread a full inch of peanutty goodness
between the slices.
"Okay, here it is," I said, as I shoved the plate her way.

I watched my sister take a bite of the heavy load
and begin to chew. She started to choke.
Coughing, hand at her throat, she fought to get
air into her windpipe. She got red in the face.

I don't remember much of what happened next.
I know that my sister survived and my team lost the game.
My sister went on to eat other meals in her life,
but none of them were ever prepared by me.

Where's Jerry?

Jerry is missing again.
He hasn't visited the birdbath
or the blazing red bougainvillia.
He hasn't looked for bugs in the wet earth.
"Jerry? Jer-ry? Jer-ry?" the birds call,
all day long.
There is no answer.
They continue searching,
calling his name.

If I went missing,
who would look for me?
Who would be first?
Would they call my name?
Drive around?
Send a text?
Just assume I'd be home by dinnertime?

That's why I love birds.
They won't rest until all loved ones
are accounted for,
until all are safe
tucked into bed.
I hope Jerry knows how lucky he is.

The Freeway Messenger

It must have been done at night.
From what I remember, there was a full moon.
It would have shone on him like a searchlight
as he leaned over the railing of the freeway bridge,
spray can in hand. Maybe a friend held his ankles.

The traffic continued under him in both directions.
Cars merged onto the 10 freeway or exited from it.
Did the passengers look up and wonder
if the guy on the bridge was about to jump?
Or did they keep driving,
turn the radio up,
forget about him?

I understand the freeway messenger.
I have messages to send too,
but I wouldn't risk my life to send them.
I once read that Adolph Wolfli,
in a mental institution, made paper airplanes
out of his writing and flew them
out the window to pedestrians below.

Our tagger risked his life to send us his message.
It took time and two colors of spray paint.
LIFE IS FULL OF B_ _ _ _ , he wrote.
The last word was shaky.
Maybe he was tired, or dizzy from spray fumes.
Maybe he heard a police siren coming.
We will never know if he wanted to tell us:
Life is Full Of Bumps, or Burps, or Bombs, or Bums.

Crying is Expected
in a Therapy Office

I used to ponder all the accumulated tears
that moistened the sofa cushions.
The side pillows too, held close,
where heads bowed in sadness.
If only those tears could talk.

The independent criers,
tears and snot streamed down.
They refused my offered kleenex,
refused to pull one of their own.
Maybe they needed to show me
how much they suffered.

The obsessive clients
tore their used tissues into pieces,
rolled them into tiny cannon balls.
Some folded and stacked them
into towers, perfect and square.

The confetti criers
celebrated a sad festivity,
tore their tissues into shreds
that littered the floor.
They knew mom would clean up after them.

The secretive ones hid.
A tissue veil
screened them
while they cried.
They needed to learn
that tears are healthy, not ugly,
not to be apologized for.

I'm retired now.
I took two of the orange side cushions
with me when I left.
I keep them and their tears close,
right here,
next to my writing desk.

Measuring the Seasons

There is a season for raspberries,
those fragile beauties –
hills and hairs on the tongue,
a purple mouth swim
in a red bathing suit.

There is a season for apples –
those practical ones,
pinching pennies in their sensible shoes,
saved in a pocket or sauced.
Very humble. No pretense.

Root vegetables have a season too,
wearing their thrift store clothing.
Hard skinned and wrinkled,
inexpensive and embarrassing,
they require a long time to do anything.

Asparagus, those sophisticated snoots,
have a short hot season.
Tall and slim, they wear couture
and speak only French.
Asparagus love a good sauce.

Alas.
I wanted to use the word *alas* in a poem.
But no *alas* is warranted here.
Like each of us, the seasons
just *are*.

The Vegetarian and the Liar

"Me too!" I said.
Why did I lie to her face?
It's true I don't eat red meat,
but that doesn't mean I'm a vegetarian.

I didn't have the heart to amend my blurted answer.
She seemed so excited to meet someone
from the food group sisterhood.

We met at a conference,
sitting under the dining tent eating lunch.
Lawnmowers buzzed around us.
My salad tasted like motor fuel and regret.

"And tonight for dinner," she told me,
"be sure to ask the food lady for the special
stuff she keeps in the back – black beans and quinoa,
corn tortillas and stuff."
"I sure will!" I said. So slippery,

my lie slid out before I had time to think.
It made me think of all the millions of the other lies
and wonder if there was a pattern to them.

Lies,
even minor ones about a lack of dietary ethics,
always have consequences.
Now, every time she's around for meals,
I only eat the buckwheat and hummus,
not the fried chicken I really want.

Do the Math

I could say more about how he sought employment,
how his scuffed satchel became stuffed with
a dark compendium of failure.
For him it was all pleasure, no business.
I could say more about laughing when he laughed,
crying when he cried.
I could say more about how we waited
for the "Sorry to inform you" letters,
the ones he stuffed in his satchel.
He was a shadow boxer, fighting
invisible gods and geniuses.
He was like an algebra problem I needed to solve.
But I had no aptitude for algebra,
the only class I ever failed.

The Girl with Stones for Eyes

Touch this dress.
None of the swimmers know you.
Can you recognize the clothing?
Run your fingers over the nap. Maybe
the smell on the jacket will move you.
Can you speak girl?

Description:
Hair black as blood.
Face, pink
as a kitten's belly.
Lips red
as plum blossoms.

Once I knew a girl like you.
She crawled from the salty sea.
Her lips couldn't form her own name.
The sea, too wild for a young one,
had its way with her.
After, it was said she was discardable.

Once I knew a girl like you.
She had stones for eyes.
That girl drowned.

On dry land.

Masked Child with a Doll, N.Y.C., 1961

photograph by DIANE ARBUS

I asked where she lived.
She pointed to the boarded up door behind her.
She sat on broken step
of scratchy concrete,
in shorts.
I imagined it felt itchy on her legs.
Her legs were dirty.
Her knees were skinned,
hair a tangled mess.
She wore sandals.
held a naked baby doll.
It was immaculate,
no hair,
no genitals,
no expression.

The girl wore a witch's mask,
hooked nose,
big snarling lips,
bent chin,
eyebrows thick and black.

I asked her why such a scary mask?
She picked at her scabbed knee.
I thought she wouldn't answer.
"It's better," she said.
"Better?" I asked.
"It's better," she said,
"to wear the scare on the outside."

Fresh Red/Stale Red

"Sonofabitch!" Mrs. Burgess said
after the speeding driver hit her car.
She'd never said that word out loud before.
Towels and laundry flew through her car.
Sheets from the bed, tiny pink bouquets,
draped over the seat.

Mrs. Burgess heard the heavy kissing of metal.
Sirens too, or was it buzzing?
She'd entered the Stanford Street/Wilshire intersection
on her way to the Bizzy Business Laundromat,
four trash bags piled on the passenger seat.
Mr. Burgess' work clothes
smelled like plaster dust and sweat.
Her head hurt a little.

This wouldn't have happened if I'd
had a proper breakfast, she thought.
"My little rabbit," her mother used to say,
"your brain can't function
without a wholesome start to the day."

Mrs. Burgess imagined being back in her driveway,
putting laundry bags on the passenger seat,
inserting her key in the ignition.
She would have eaten some Irish oats
with blueberries and sipped a cup of black tea.
She wouldn't have known
a reckless speeder was out there,
looking for her car,
looking for her,
looking for a stale red light.

Remodeling My Heart

All of it dragged me down.
Down the incline of 20th Street.
Down the asphalt sidewalk.
Down the slope of slips,
down to the depths of down.

The orange shag carpet remained.
The palm tree, regal,
outside the window,
wore its red necklace.
My brother's portrait nailed to the wall:
his eyes watched the overwatered ivy
escape the terrarium.

I didn't want to leave.
I kicked my legs.
I was afraid.
Dug in my heels,
created a scene,
grabbed at bushes
held on to car antennas.

It dragged me down.
Down the incline of 20th Street.
Down the asphalt sidewalk.
Down the slope of slips.
Down to the depths of down.

Sometimes,
a key needs
to unlock
a quiet door.
A safe door.
The door to nothing in particular.
Like for instance,
matching green dishes.
A skillet with a lid.
A TV with four channels.
A long, quiet sleep
on a pillowcase
embroidered with vintage flowers.

2

MY BODY THE BILLBOARD

Nude Descending a Staircase
Without Laundry

I wish he would wait,
just once,
at the bottom landing.
I'd glide down the stairs nude.
No stained apron,
no shabby bathrobe.
No laundry basket on a hip.
No squirmy infant under my arm.

Always in a hurry,
pixelated joints pumping,
knees lifting, my
efficient movement creates
a breeze in the stairwell.
Head down,
thinking about the mortgage,
I feel as worn as the old carpet
on the treads.

If he was waiting,
just once,
I would take my time,
head held high.
I would find my footing again,
and walk with assured,
naked grace,
wearing only bright red lipstick,
down the old staircase.

Sexual Hygiene

His cigarette glowed in the dark like a sore.
We were waiting to consummate our marriage.
Friends said be patient, but for how many days?
We were lying on our new bed, staring
at the cracks in the ceiling, hoping
they would spell out sexual instructions.
Above the ceiling, the sky fell away
to reveal an orgy of stars.

My husband slept in his clothes:
heavy workshirt with cargo pockets,
pants, belt and socks.
I had never seen him naked.
I wore the filmy blue lace peignoir
my grandmother bought for the wedding night.

I checked out books from the library
on sexual hygiene.
I studied the diagrams of male and female organs.
I considered the suggestions on what husbands' like:
feminine attire, frequent showers,
makeup and good grooming,
soft tones, hot meals,
inquiries about his day.

But those books didn't help. I needed
a handbook on hydraulics, or better yet,
geometry:
How do I make two curves fit together?
How many sides are there to an angle?
How do I circle the square?

He smoked. I breathed it in.
It was the most intimate exchange we had.

We might still be lying there, staring at the ceiling
in our mismatched outfits
if he hadn't decided to leave me,
travel to New York City,
become a jazz saxophonist.
He didn't know how to play the saxophone
but he told me that didn't matter.
It was a time of great possibility, he said,
and anything could happen.

First Apartment

I was 20. It happened.
Tomatoes and squash grew in the garden.
Baked potato and spam, cooking.
Television tuned to the news.
Traffic going by on Fourteenth Street.
My first apartment happened.
My own little oven, my fireplace.
Cleaning all day happened.
My first bath in my own tub happened.
A stranger's eyes sparkled, watched me
through the crack of my bathroom door.
I screamed. That happened too.

Later, the Police asked why I screamed.
Why hadn't I acted normal?
Dried myself off with a towel,
strolled to the bedroom naked?
Why hadn't I acted normal?
Called them on my rotary phone?
Dressed slowly, a reverse strip tease?
They would have come, they said,
they could have arrested him.
All that didn't occur to me.

I was an unbaked cinnamon bun on a hot pan.
I was a newborn puppy.
I was a lily bending in the heat.
I was a scream I didn't know I had.
I was only 20.
It happened.
It wasn't normal.

The Organ of Principal Interest

If Freud had bothered to ask what I envied,
I would have told him
my sister's majorette baton.
Shiny silver, rubber knobs on each end
with triangle engravings for good grip.
I twirled figure eights in front of the mirror.
I envied her costumes too,
white ankle boots with pom poms,
shorts with sequins,
midriff top and sparkly headband.

Penis Envy was a thing I studied in grad school.
I memorized the various stages,
those endured by males
and the misfortune of unendowed females.
Picture a veritable lunar calendar.
A penis stands solidly in the center
while female moons orbit around it.
Both males and females
seemed equally obsessed with the penis.
The anxiety of discovering you didn't have one!
The insecurity,
the knotted sexual desire,
the misplaced aggressive drive,
the thwarted desire to seduce the parent,
the desire to castrate those born with one.

I wasn't asked if I wanted to be a baton twirler.
It was my sister's thing, they said, not mine.
But if I had become a famous baton twirler,
I wouldn't have gone to grad school.
I wouldn't have learned about penis envy.
And while I smirk at the silly theory,
I remember that Freud also
discovered the unconscious mind.
So who's to say
there's not a lonely penis
lurking somewhere in mine.

To the Man Who Grabs Girls

You want to plow me –
a crop
you didn't plant,
bite me
like bits of ripe tomato
on toast, my two yolks
sun up,
young and fresh.

After all,
young girls
are like breakfast.
Hot. Fragrant.
Hominy on a plate.
Innocent corn
that did nothing
to deserve your
little flypaper hands.

The Difference
Between Falling and Flying

I never kissed Karl,
but he shared his sandwich with me once.
I was 11. He was a man of 15.

I never took off my clothes for Karl,
but I thought I would,
under his grape arbor, dripping with sugar.

Karl never touched me
except when he dragged me
up the stairs to his pigeon coop.

I heard them flutter and coo,
Karl's homing pigeons,
trained to fly home.
They wore silver bracelets on their scaly ankles.

Karl never hurt me
but on the roof, his eyes got funny
when he said my name.
He said I did things to his body.

Karl leaned close and told me what
he did to his sister. I stopped thinking
about taking my clothes off,
and thought instead of cages, and being lost.

I still remember
the taste of those purple grapes
and his name, Karl.
Karl with a K.

Conversation at MUSSO AND FRANK'S

"What kind of train are you?" I asked him.

Upon reaching the advanced stage of a relationship,
a couple can run out of things to talk about.
We were at a fancy restaurant for his birthday dinner.
To our left was a newlywed couple.

"How do you know they're newlyweds?" he asked.
"It's so obvious!" I said.

They were having champagne and lobster,
sitting close together in the booth,
and they were *talking* to each other.
Listen! That was a major tipoff!

"What kind of *train* am I?" he repeated.
His eyebrows did that incredulous questioning thing,
like maybe I needed a psychiatric evaluation.
I watched as an oyster cracker floated by on my chowder.

"Yeah, given your personality, if you were a train,
what kind would you be?"

"I would be a plush car on the Orient Express," he said.
"Red velvet seats,
tiger lilies abiding in a vase,
the gravity of starched uniforms,
seafood swimming in a bowl of crushed ice."

"I would be a freight car," I said,
"carrying bars of iron.
I would be strong.
My effort would create structure,
would make others happy."

All those bars of iron, all that weight, I thought.
I pictured soiled laundry piled as high as Mt. Kilimanjaro,
enough hard boiled eggs to fill a swimming pool,
dirty dishes that stretched out my window to the sea.

I cut a bite of meat
and with weary arms, lifted
the bloody morsel to my lips.

The Woman
Who Climbed the Water Tower

Some things I know and some things I don't.
I know it was a very hot afternoon.
Hot enough for us to wear sandals
and shorts, to poke tar bubbles
in the gutter with sticks.
We were waiting for the Good Humor Man
and Double Buddy popsicles.

"Look! There's someone on the water tower!"
I don't know who said it first.
I didn't even know it was a woman
till Karl got his binoculars.
She was on the very top
like an ant on an aluminum pan.

How scary to climb that thin ladder,
up the side to the rounded peak.
My mother whisked us inside, so I guessed
the woman wasn't up there to take a picture.

I never learned how she got down.
There was nothing in the Evening Outlook
and my parents weren't talking.
But I heard she took her Bible with her.
When I heard that, something in me cracked,
broke and fell away.

Uncle Murray's Business

They said Uncle Murray was good with his hands.
This explained why he didn't talk much.
I can't even remember his voice.

They said Uncle Murray worked out of the home,
which meant he worked at home, not out.
Uncle Murray worked on naked women.

In his back room was a leather table covered with paper.
No Entry! said the sign on the door. Keep Out!
Sometimes I peeked through the opening door.

Uncle Murray shot and killed the squirrely hairs
on naked women's bodies with an electric machine.
He went to shooting school for a certificate in hair killing.

The women entered by the back porch,
passed the washer and dryer that tumbled Uncle Murray's
socks and underwear. The women could smell
Tilly's brisket cooking, onions in schmaltz and gefilte fish.

They said each hair needed many treatments.
The human pincushions left covered with red dots,
proof that Uncle Murray hit his hairy targets.

Uncle Murray was *too* good with his hands, they said later.
Some customers got more than smooth chins and thighs.
After Tilly and Aunt Sylvia found out,
Uncle Murray packed up his table and I never saw him again.

Love, Plumbing, and Flex Coupling

My darling bull nose hot mop!
Other ball joints come and go
but you, my sexy dip tube,
will stay in my heart like sediment.

I met you when I was a young flapper.
My valves and elbows were clean.
I wasn't looking then
for compression or flex coupling.

Be my water hammer, my dearest,
a ball cock to call my very own!
Let's stand as firm as green board,
move our backflow forward,
and make beautiful gray water, together!

The Evolution of a Pickle

Gender can be the maybe between yes and no,
the baseball suspended between bases,
the loose change in the Tips jar.

We are sitting on the patio
talking about them,
the fluid fugue entered in college.

The red and white Bougainvillia hangs
on the garage like droopy streamers
from an ancient prom.
Sitting in the warm sunshine,
I think of pickles.
There is no definition for the precise moment
a cucumber becomes a pickle.
It's a pause between notes,
time for alchemy to do its work.
Sometimes there's an intermission.

I picture a raft floating
between unnamed islands.
Eventually there has to be a destination, right?
Or there may be a pause in pickling brine,
between the cucumber that once was
and whatever will come next.

Crevasse

Some days in the fall,
the walls,
like human skin,
get thinner.

On these days,
the membrane between
the living and the dead stretches,
as if the skull of a lost one
is pushing through.

Across the open air,
the so-what-ness of trees
by the vacant lot
serve as reminders
of more stable things.

No one wakes up one morning
and thinks this is the day
I will fall out of love.
Erosion, drips of water
on solid rock,
crevasse and canyon,
drip and drip and carve,
until his sleepy eyes
persuade me no longer.

It's like this.
When people ask me what happened,
I tell them it was fall,
it was life or death,
it was the dripping water.

Let Me Count the Ways

We were like, you might say,
crossed swords.
On foggy mornings,
I think of him
with death on my tongue.

I'd like to poke my sword
into his unfortunate sweater vest.
Under it, his robust body stands
ready to push somebody around.

Or maybe,
we were a hangman's noose.
My neck itches when I remember.
His sheets smelled like gasoline.
His lips tasted like arson.

We were pistols at daybreak.
We walked four paces away then turned.
His arm straightened as he aimed
for my red paper heart.

I still cry about him once in a while,
but only from one eye.
That's all I can manage.
That's all he deserves.

Because Paris

I stack my clothes on the bed. Because
I missed you after work. Because
I answered my texts instead. Because
I was afraid to come home. Because
we'd been fighting. Because
you drink too much and get jealous. Because
I've given you plenty of reasons. Because
you don't pay enough attention to me.

Your letter said Paris.
I want to go to Paris,
be sophisticated.
I want to see the sights. Paris.
The name of the city, so romantic. Paris.
The city of lovers, Paris.
I would share my crepe with you.
I would go to Café Flore with you.
I would walk over the river bridge with you.
Your missing suitcase says you are elsewhere.
And I'm stuck here in Akron.

Too Much Normal

A pile of clothes, under
the empty moon.
Breadcrumbs lead to where
the forest memory held us close,
two chemical elements, our skins
rubbed together to make fire.

All I ever wanted was everything.

But now I walk in the earthly sun.
I am a mailbox. I am a lemon tree.
I buy cereal in bulk.
I'm a quiet house on a normal street,
where a good man comes home.

I shed my burning skin long ago.
Now I am one chemical element
with no explosion.
But I still wear us like a black tattoo,
an empty moon over a tree,
etched in a secret place.
It has faded
from so much sunlight,
from so much normal.

My Marlin

Hudson's leash is looped over my wrist
and grasped by my full hand for security.
I pull my jacket closer against the cold morning.
I'm probably staring at the full moon,
or noting the new graffiti on the building
where that artist guy hung himself years ago.
Maybe I am wondering which tree is *the* one.

I must have loosened my grip.
Around the corner bounds a huge dog.
Hudson jerks and I let go.
It could have been certain death,
but the huge dog is wearing a muzzle--
already a convicted felon I guess.
There is bumping and squealing,
but this morning , no one dies.

This makes me think of you.
I'm trying to keep you safe too.
You are at the end of a slim filament,
my pole is bent with effort.
You thrash in the water like a marlin,
spray and waves in your wake.
Like Hudson's leash, I feel the line jerk
and I watch as you begin
to slip through my fingers.

Two Toads

The rifles that lined his wall
didn't make me leave.
When he called me his gutter ball I didn't leave.
When he cut my bangs as I slept,
when he brought home food for himself
but not for me.
when I fell down the stairs and he laughed,
I didn't leave.

But when I saw the two toads
nailed above the front door, I left.
I ran across the pavement like road kill,
got in my car, turned my music
up real loud.

I drove down that tobacco road
saying my goodbyes to the wooden shacks.
I passed the water tower that said Hicksonville.
I drove past the church where he said
he would marry me.
I drove past Dora's Café and past the Grange Hall.
I drove past the Laundromat with
the machines that swallowed my coins.

I drove down that hot tar road
under the blue preaching tent of a sky.
I drove past the corn doing what corn does.
As I drove down that godforsaken road,
I rolled up the white lane strip behind me,
like rolling a white ribbon from a gift.
I didn't know where I was going,
but I figured without that strip he'd never find me.

How to Make It Rain

Wake up the pips.
Place them near
the warmth of the sun
on a cloudless day.
It needn't take long.

If the underbelly of the sky
is ripe and proficient,
and if an itching begins there,
a linkage of pleats and tubes
will occur in an hour or less.

If the mouth of the sky
is shaped like time
as it whispers secrets to
the green grass,
get out your umbrella.

Once the hidden rags of moisture
get acquainted
with the pellets of wind,
and meet on the corner with
the prayers of dusty children,

rain will fall
from the sky
like a silken robe
begins to fall over the shoulders
of a thirsty woman.

Night Disease

I tap my phone.
Greenish light haloes my hand.
The clock reads 2:30.
I shake out my boots – no spiders –
go out into the yard.
It's a slow motion night.
No stars, no breeze.
My nightgown sticks to my skin.
The moon pushes against the clouds,
trying to be seen.
The air feels like soup,
cooked slow in an enclosed kitchen.
If he was here, I would say,
"What a night!"
Instead I go back inside,
open the tap,
drink a glass of water.
I hold the phone, hoping for a buzz or a ding,
hoping for a call,
hoping for a chance to say
"I really messed up."
Rain begins to tap on the roof.
Then it knocks.
Then it hammers.
"What a night,"
I say out loud to no one.

Fingers of Death

My mother killed them all.
The *Adenium obesum.*
The *Ficus elastica.*
The *Sansevieria metallica.*
They all ended up as dust
in the compost heap.

The pile of empty containers
in her garage grew.
The red tin with the Reindeer
and snowflakes.
The clay Easter bunny.
The glass globe for the terrarium.
The white pot with valentine hearts.

She overwatered.
She neglected.
She overfed.
She didn't know how to love them.

Somewhere on the way to her address,
the plants lost their will to live.
They slumped over dead
before they arrived.
I believe that sometimes they
threw themselves over her porch railing,
choosing to take matters into
their own hands, (so to speak)
rather than face her torture.

I knew how they felt.
The day after high school ended,
this Homo sapiens femina
jumped out her bedroom window
and ran for her life.

Kimchi Fried Rice

Where naked chicken breasts
sat in repose every other night,
a bubbling deforestation project sat instead.
A blazing fire pot.
A volcanic fusion of funk.
A cauldron of atomic goodness.

Orange smoke,
the kind magicians use
when they pull a white dove
out of a secret compartment,
blew through, hot and dry.
The wooden cabinets breathed in,
coughed a little,
and remembered the scent.

Vegetables were added:
shitaki mushrooms, spinach,
onions, garlic, peas, broccoli.
Master KimChi,
hands on hips like Yul Brenner
in The King and I,
pointed and laughed.

KimChi
doesn't hide from anyone,
is an extrovert,
doesn't sneak up on you,
has been told to tone down,
wears orange and red. Together.
KimChi may be a Scorpio.

When I washed my face for bed,
I felt renewed, worldly, travelled.
Like life itself had snuck up on me.
I smiled into the mirror.

Do Not Play Dominoes
the Night You Die

Death is a career, not a game or hobby.
Curses and strikes of lightning can be expected.
Clouds will scurry forth and dress the moon in a fuzzy frock.
Look upward, meteors will spell out which game is best.

Hopscotch maybe.
The coins and lost teeth will rattle in your pocket as you jump,
sounding like beans in a gourd,
marking time to a last rhumba.

Avoid the Ouija board. The big questions
have already been answered.
A songbook could be nice but avoid
Christmas songs that remind you of
family. Why aren't they here, anyway?

Leap from your bed with ballet arms!
Shake your hips like you are Elvis.
Remove your pants under God's supervision.
Your clothing will be removed soon anyway.
Raise those jazz hands to the sun that may not rise again.

I think it's someone's birthday today but not mine.
Let the candles on their cake burn with a fury
as I flame out in a frenzy of my own.
I will curse and dance with every pulse
until I snuff my candle out
and journey into the dying light.

Dirt Angels

We lie in the dirt,
two women making dirt angels,
two grownups holding hands.
We laugh as cars drive by.

We look at the sky
for pictures,
for messages,
for direction,
for entertainment.
A car honks,
we laugh harder.

We were in St. Helena,
the land of wine and meadows.
Her middle name was Helena.
She was my saint.
She suffered like a saint later.

Now I'm in Los Angeles.
I lie in the dirt alone.
I look up for a sign.
I am not laughing.
I am not a saint.

The clouds are rimmed with black.
They dance and speed,
form a galloping bison,
a house on fire,
a line of handwriting blown loose.

My own Saint Helena draws
cotton candy pictures for me.
First a turtle with three legs.
Next a wedding veil.
And before the wind loosens
a line of handwriting
that reads:
I miss you.

How to Rescue a Marriage with Fruit

I place green slices
of star fruit on his eyes.
We pretend he has departed,
I say sad prayers over his body,
then he sits up and declares
"I'm alive!"

We wear pineapple top hats,
fascinators,
and try to make each other laugh.

Bananas and cherimoyas
make interesting shadow puppets.
We produce the Story of Creation
on our bedroom wall.
Our hands touch.

I feed him peeled grapes one at a time,
to make him feel special.
We sew matching raisin necklaces.

Wearing only a coconut bra
I walk into the living room
where he is staring into middle earth.
"Is this sexy?" I ask.

We are the stirred fruit
on the bottom of a cocktail glass.
We squash a ripe tamarind
between our rock-hard abs.
Juice drools onto the sheets,
puddling there.
Seeds stick to our skin
like the road markers of our many years.

The Flesh Near the Pit

Hold my hand.
In these minutes under the bleachers,
we are prowlers in my mother's holy garden.
My pink pants are photogenic
against your starched white shirt.

The script may be new
but my hands know the lines.
Our folly blooms on the ride upward
and on the hard water landing.
Our sport is summer, played under
the bleachers where the grass is brown.

Heat scrapes on a nerve.
Far away boys practice other sports
and we hear shouts and footfalls.
While I look into your eyes,
rocks heave and moons eclipse.
The flesh nearest the pit
is always the sweetest.

Hold my hand.
Under the bleachers,
I do not fear the bad blood of summer.
No, I fear that voice in the distance
my mother calling my name,
my mother calling me home to dinner.

The Fickle Ocean

The ocean thinks
it can roll in and out
any time it damn pleases.
It crashes on my mile of shadows,
hugs my ragged edge
without a thought for me.

The faithless ocean,
with its clammy hands,
grabs, sprays and thumps.
The ocean has no limits.
It shows off,
tests how big it can go,
applauds itself,
then leaves only bubbles behind.

The ocean thinks it's the boss,
that it can roll over me anytime
before it heads for the blue horizon.

Stupid me,
enchanted and dizzy,
I forget my tongue.
I forget my rights.
I settle for the coming
and forget that the going will follow.

Love is a Refugee

I'm in the backseat of the car, on my way to Sorrento Beach.
Hamburgers drive me on,
and a faded red surfrider steered with a rope. I take
the long ride to shore before the waves crash.
Every time, I risk a broken neck.

My fears from childhood:
the electric radio falling into the bathtub;
a broken neck by ocean waves or shallow pool;
rogue whales;
quicksand.

You remind me of a seagull with one leg.
I watch you, my sister, limb extended,
showing off, posing on the sand.
Your blonde curls get blonder in the sun.
You peck for sand crabs with your baby shovel.
I watch you in your ruffled bathing suit, laughing.
I eat my burger from Neeny's on the sand.
Morose.

I feared all the wrong things in childhood.
Life taught me what to really fear.
I learned that home is not always safe.
Love is a refugee. And, I mean,
that sometimes being yourself
is just the wrong thing to be.

Summer Juice

Remember the time I waded out,
burning thighs,
into the cool water?
Fish leapt into my birthday air.
The sand cradled my long feet
and took my vital signs.

Remember the time I ran
ahead of my face into the sea?
I wanted to fly like a fish.
I wanted my shadow to flash green
against the water.

Remember the time my mouth was drowsy?
I wanted to close my eyes in the heat.
My eyes were heavy with dreams.
I wanted to eclipse the sun
with my own skin,
my own skin,
covered with a million burning flowers.

My Chubby Legs on a Piano Bench

"It will make you popular at parties," my mother said.
I didn't want lessons.
I liked tinkering,
making up chords and songs
while my feet swung loose.
I couldn't reach the pedals.
"You will have to practice thirty minutes a day.
I'm not paying for lessons if you don't practice."
I didn't want lessons.
Keep your money, I thought.
Leave me alone, I thought.
She didn't listen.

I fired my first teacher.
She was old and mean.
We met at her stinky house.
While she was in the bathroom,
I walked out.
Mother made me go back to apologize.

My second teacher was a college man.
My mother insisted he teach me
Cocktails For Two,
so I could entertain her potluck peers.
My fingers learned the song but my brain didn't.
Teacher number two got drafted and went to war.

There was no third teacher.
My mother didn't learn to listen,
she just gave up.
And for the record,
I never once went to a party
where a piano was present.
My friends had fancy stereos.
I never played my one song for anyone
except Mom and her drunken friends.
And furthermore Mom,
I was plenty popular without a piano.
So popular with the boys in fact,
it created a shitload of trouble
that you could constantly
bother me about.

Atonal Music

You talk about Hadrian's Villa,
You talk about how cursive writing
can build synapses in the brain.

I talk about Real Housewives
of various cities.
I talk about Tupac's killer
still on the loose.

In restaurants,
we are often silent.
I don't want to hear about the book
you're reading on atonal music.
You don't want to hear about
the memoir I'm reading
about an addicted mother.

But when we lie in bed in the morning,
dog under the blanket,
coffee on our side tables,
double doors flung open to the yard,
to the Japanese magnolia bought as our first Valentine,
the red climbing rose,
the doves in the birdbath,
we both, for once,
appreciate the same thing.

.

I Miss Their Fluids

I remember the Creamsicle
melting in my favorite purse.
The number of soiled onesies
I laundered in a day,
the washer humping,
my looped boombox.
What do these kids do to get so dirty?
They're too little to dig tunnels,
fight fires, serve soup in a restaurant,
or repair leaking pipes.

I miss the milk burp on my shoulder.
Strained apricots on the bib, more out than in.
Pee squirted during a change.
Sneezes soiling my shirt.
Sticky spilled lemonade.

Sharing their fluids, so intimate.
When we weren't too tired,
we adults would laugh
at the mess of life.

Now they share little, growing
into their outlines on a different coast.
They give us only broad themes,
one sentence news:
Nothing.
Fine.
Okay.

No details.
No mess.
No intimacy.

Lessons from the Mothership

Last night, I dreamed I cooked him pears.
I worry I'm a bad wife.
But my Mothership taught me
nothing about marriage.

This morning as he was making coffee, he whistled
Just Friends-Lovers No More. I knew I was failing.
He broadcasts his marital feelings by the tune he whistles.
I want to keep my inside track open so I don't
share this observation.

We're just making this marriage thing up as we go along.
We are like softened soap fragments formed into a ball.
We are like iced tea and lemonade on the rocks.
We are like two bald tires going in the same direction.

Our role models?
Hostage takers, blackmailers, drunks, those beaten about
the face and eyes, deprivers, starvationists, needy babies,
flirties, raspberry smashers, deluxe druggers, emotional anorexics,
hypo fill-in-the-blankers, complainers,
glass shatterers, suburbanites living in the city, animal haters, make
you feel smallaholics, affection celibates, shallow ditch diggers,
icecube heads, hungrybelly mooners, forehead
frowners, circle walkers and seduction soda jerks.
So, Whoa Nelly, what do you expect?

I will cook him some pears.
I want to get arrested for snuggling.
I want to tell him to whistle a happier tune,
and that I love him with my everything.

Gun Safety

After the gun is pointed at my head,
I understand.
The wind fits into my pocket.
The lights go on.
I can smell kindness.
The moon is waiting for me.
The dogs understand my verbs.
Fire is my friend.
I stitch love into the lining of my jacket.
I take the slow train.
I taste things.
I catalog every kiss.
Sap runs back into the tree.
Paradise is a cello playing in the background.
Paradise is the bullet backing up into the gun.

My Illuminated Manuscript

The dermatologist came at me
with her ice wand,
leaving me no time to reflect
upon the layers of my face,
stained like an old library book.

I needed to say goodbye
to the unclosed blinds,
the cigar stubs,
the motor oil used to tan faster.
Goodbye to the whispered invitations,
the diving board,
the enchanted trees,
the rubberized bathing suit
with the baby white underneath.

I needed to say goodbye to
learning to surf,
the taste of salt on my skin,
the hurricane shutters,
the swaddled towel,
being buried alive,
to hot bologna sandwiches
and ripe plums.

All the bumps in my past,
the unsmooth edges,
the stains,
were expunged.
I was cleared of all charges.
Yet, beneath the redemption,
the illuminated memories
continue to burn.

The Bones Beneath the Bones

This is for the bones
and the bones beneath the bones.
My body is called
The Fish Of Air,
delicate to the taste
except for the thread-like bones
that catch in the throat of the
unsuspecting.

This is for the bones
and the red pumping things
beneath the bones.
The inners of my body are called
The Sacred Globes.
They are not fooling around.
The shiny slippery things,
in my favorite shades of burgundy and red,
do the hard work few notice.

This is for the bones,
and the red pumping things
beneath the bones.
And this is for the seaman's coiled ropes
in the place called The Helmet's Cave,
that gray, buzzing, synapse place
of a million stinging bees
where burning data is transmitted
through cables of velvet
by lightening bolts.

This is a thank you to the fragile envelope
called The Hairless Tent.
This covering of paper tissue
protects the delicate bones,
the pumping things,
and the buzzing coils.
The whole package, a gift,
has been unwrapped
and is gratefully accepted
as the long term loan it is.

My Old Pocketbook

"It's shriveling nicely," the gynecologist said.
He was referring to my uterus.
I pictured a wrinkled leather handbag,
left in the sun for too many decades.

The gynecologist seemed very excited
about this development,
about the tricks
my postmenopausal uterus was playing.
"It's now the size of a small gray pear,"
he said as we congratulated each other.

But,
walking to my car
across the hot asphalt,
I kept thinking
of a wrinkled
gray hand
closing
around feathers,
and sand,
and empty air.

What Fruit or Vegetable Are You?

The Facebook quiz warned me about getting my hopes up.
"Everyone wants to be a tomato," it said,
"but only eight percent of respondents are tomatoes."

While the quiz was preparing my answer,
I thought of common fruits and vegetables,
seeking one with a feeling of familiarity.

Maybe I'm a zucchini,
common, cheap, kind of bland,
but zucchini can always be spiced up
and made more saucy.

Or maybe I'm a raisin,
a cabernet grape with low expectations,
skin wrinkled from lack of sunscreen
on many long summer days.

Or maybe I'm a carrot.
My hair looks orange in certain light,
plumes sprouting willy nilly.
A carrot has a wrinkled complexion
and grows occasional wild hairs.

My quiz results popped onto the screen:
Without even reading the explanation,
I understood why it said I am a hubbard squash.

"Hubbard squash are covered with a hard,
almost inpenetrable shell.
But once cracked open,
the flesh inside this versatile vegetable
is usually soft and sweet."

The Splintered Root

A conveyor belt delivers mutton and fowl.
Hot meringues suffer and collapse
under my ruthless fork.
Fish swim through bubbles of fat to get to me.
Pancakes topple and burn my fingers.
If I keep eating I won't think of her.

The memory of her is like oil and vinegar,
years of bitter salad.
There was no juice in her lemon
so I just kept squeezing.
A man in love is a man on fire,
his burning eyes, hot pools of syrup.

Now I stand alone, naked,
a red splintered root.
I keep eating to forget her.
I eat things that burn my tongue
because my frozen wife left me
with a stomach full of snow.

A Paper Girl

They call it the dinette.
I sit there alone,
thinking of the stones
that fill my body.
When I move,
I hear them knock and split.

I pretend I am a mountain.
I pretend I am a trail
leading away.
I pretend my body is strong,
a weapon.

I want to go to the piano,
to the framed photograph,
take the safety scissors,
cut my picture out, leaving
a hole among the other faces.

But that is just pretend.
I am real. A real cut-out hole,
a negative space.
A paper girl.
I am just a tiny pile of sand.

The Miniature Letter

Dearheart, How shall I find you?

Mouth like a ripple on a lake,
chin shaped like a leaf,
nose a swoop of smoke.

Between your eyes,
one larger than the other,
is a tiny letter to me.

The writing is small.
I have squinted hard
with glasses and without.

If I could decipher your letter,
I think it would tell me
you are obsessed with
knives and forks.
It would speak of your desire to form
a square with perfectly
equal sides,
of your need to clean up a mess
if it is slippery,
and your love of pinkish shrubs.

I wish to tell you
that you are beautiful
in the pitch of darkness
when the drafts of sleep
fall upon you.

Dearheart, you are not
misunderstood by others.
No. You are misunderstood
by yourself alone.

My Body the Billboard

The man in the moon looked up my skirt,
touched me with moist fingers.
He understood the buttons on my sweater.
The bellows of cool air,
broached my skin
as I was opened.

I was a package,
unwrapped
and wrapped again
in used, wrinkled paper.
It was never *my* birthday,
I was just a present for the multitudes.
But instead of a loaf or a fish,
there was only me.

You're on My Mind

You are flour and water.
I am the mahogany pit
inside a loquat.

You are a lipstick blot on a tissue.
I am the convulsing mouth
that tries to kiss you.

My mind is filled with thugs,
and tripping stones. I sail alone
on tangled foreign oceans
but I know I will survive
because love is a rational disease.

Jungle Girl

Her name was Morgan.
She had bangs that stuck to her
forehead like shingles on a roof.
Her hair smelled like an animal pelt.
Morgan gathered branches on her
way to school. She rescued
wounded animals at night.

Her enemies, the bullies,
Rufus, Unruh and Amfar,
mocked her branches,
called her jungle girl.
They said she smelled like a rodent
and released the animals she caught.

Every Easter, when spring shimmered
in the heartland and the fruit trees blossomed,
Morgan prayed for an Easter miracle.
She wanted to push over the heavy stone
that weighed her down, like in the Bible.
She prayed that Rufus, Unruh and Amfar
would be given kind hands and sweet mouths.
If this failed, Morgan prayed for
a sharp magical sword to replace her sticks.

I Heart You

Your eyes are not enchanted pools that skirt the river.
They are just eyes.

Your nose is not a letter that never arrived at my door.
It is just a nose.

Your mouth is not a scrap of paper inscribed with secrets,
or a mound of crushed berries atop a meringue.
It is just a mouth.

But this morning,
when I overheard you wish our dogs a Happy New Year,
ask if they
made any resolutions,
petals fell upon my heart
and I knew you were mine.

A Poem About Losing My Virginity
and My Moral Compass

It was time.
I stopped going to confession, started
reading the Constitution.
All that freedom shit,
my own Bill Of Rights.
Anyway,
I was also reading lyrics
from Downbound Train,
looking for direction,
looking for advice.

It was New Year's.
I was gonna be a new me.
I found a younger neighbor kid.
I wasn't gonna be passive, a passenger
on that Downbound Train,
so I put on my puffy blue and white
engineer's hat,
the Woo Woo whistle blowing in my head.
I led him into our recreation room.
(We called it the Wreck Room.)
And none of your business.
The End.

Lifespan of Men

Start with a bucket of sighs.
Hook that bucket on a sappy tree
where it will suck in
water,
oxygen,
and sun.
Green growth will conceal
(for a while)
what's underneath.
Leaves, the fated offspring,
will fly away as soon as possible.
Left behind is
brown,
scratchy
wilderness.

The Lunch Was My Idea

overheard dialog

It's a wig.
I feel like Robert Durst.
It's giving me a headache.
I'll be sixty-three this year.
Can we buzz it?
I go to a vegetarian barber.
I'll go with anything hip or cool.
I'm drenched in sweat.
Going rogue would feel good.
Can I eat my lunch in here?
Yes.

He's a real writer.
I could have told you that, man.
We should've been here years ago.
Yes!
A million billion.
Yes. He knows the tango.
And the cha cha cha.
He directs her to go two inches shorter.
Instead she cuts the door 6 x 7.
Throw out an emotion.
Any emotion.
Mine is: A Jamaican guy says, so cool
you love your mother so much.
Okay.
How about:
A rending of garments?

Just Ate a Donut
and I'm Sweating with Happiness

overheard dialog

I'm like,
what the hell?
My phone and my butt are too big.
I was just thinking that too!
But I won't get involved.
Water? I don't want to have a heart attack.
Gonna keep my two hands on my binder.
I was just thinking that too!

This is cool, like a museum.
I know!
We can sit. We can do anything,
anything we set our minds to.
I was just thinking that too!
So he said to me…
Yeah?
Have you ever been down there?
Oh no!
She could find places to do that?

I hear it's all about the screenplay.
I hear radiation gives her power.
She's somebody's special child.
All these people I don't know.
Yeah.
So much stuff here.
Oh gosh I can't imagine.
I'm like,
I guess she wants to be popular.
I was just thinking that too!

To an Unnamed Husband

I want to be your landslide.
I want to be the rubble in your shoe.
I want to be the smell you can't forget,
the dust you can't wash off.

I'd like to roll up your hairy sleeves,
investigate every wrinkle and scar,
learn braille and read
the mayhem of your story.

I want to adopt your brand,
cut a hole in it,
slip it over my head.
I want to review
the brand of you online,
award it five stars,
give it a thumbs up.

I want to bump over your long legs
like a broken lawnmower,
examine every inch
while we lie in the hot sand
under the yellow, yellow sun.

I want to be a butterfly
in your pocket.
I want to hold your butterfly-hand
and fly away with you
when the landslide
begins to fall around us.

We Met at the Corner of
Known and Unknown

Him: blonde, with crisp vitals.
Me: a clammy redhead with a dream of roses.
Us: slim ribbons of common sense.

We hugged on jagged rims
along canyons of shadows.
If there is something that describes
being blinder than blind,
that was us.

Above, the sky was a tumbling radiance.
Stars of all sizes blinked their approval.
I hibernated in his warmth.
I swam his tributaries.
I tasted the flesh of his oranges.
I paid good alms for my fortune

Our love deepened,
spread like ink on a pond.
We smelled the earth together,
together we deemed it good.
We decided our love would last
until the moon crashed into the mountains.

Now we live
at the corner of known and known.
Now in our garden,
the roses bloom.

Some Things Are Obvious

If you want to measure foot traffic,
look at the linoleum.

To multiply Here times There,
your fingers can't do the job.

To welcome a visitor,
unlock your metaphor.

To learn to cook,
you must boil your trout.

To attract a boy,
go upside down on the jungle bars.

To live a life without pain,
learn robotics.

Oh my dearest fruity-tooty,
my toasted lemon bar,
my butter fluff,
my sugar helium balloon,

some things *are* obvious.

Like the word devotion
for example,
and my smile
when I say your name.

Cranberry

She was an innocent cranberry,
a Sixth Grader wading into a new year.
She tried to open her combination lock.
Three numbers memorized,
left spin, right spin, left spin.
Pull. Nothing.

In the September heat wave,
she wore a grey sweater and skirt set,
new whitey-white saddle shoes
that creaked when she walked,
and a cotton bra that couldn't support
a three cent envelope.

She wanted to decorate her locker
like the cool girls did,
with celebrities – but which ones?
In the cafeteria, she watched
the popular girls flip their hair and laugh,
showing their teeth.
She copied what others ate, tried to keep
dishes from sliding off the tray
as she found an empty place to sit.

Boys seemed interested in her sweater set
and in the thin bra underneath.
Boys became her collateral
so she majored in boys.
Sometimes they slipped dirty notes
into her locker,
drawings of body parts and
words she didn't understand.
Standing in front of her locker,
decorated with kittens and glittery stars,
she studied those notes
as if they were her homework.

117

The Daydream

It was the night the fog rolled in.
I wandered alone in the forest,
grateful no one was talking to me.
The moon wore her white robes,
streaks of light escaped under her hem.
My gown was like a goblet of scarlet wine.
Moisture beaded on the skirt like jewels.
I was lost in time until I heard a sound
from the darkness between the trees.
I took off my hat, shook the dew from the wide brim.
I heard the sound again. . .

"Where did you go?" he asked.
"What? Oh, sorry, " I said. "I was lost in thought."
He stood next to me wearing a women's bathrobe
he bought at a thrift store.
He hadn't shaved.
A shriveled green pea from dinner lay on the floor.
"I'm used to you not paying attention to what I say," he said.
I was standing next to a sinkful of dirty dishes.
It was my turn.
He was stirring coffee in his favorite chipped cup.
He hadn't poured one for me.
The spoon made a clinking sound around the rim of the cup.
I wondered if he was trying to hypnotize me
like in the movie "Get Out."
"I wish things were different," he said.
"Me too," I said.
He thought I meant I wanted to become a better listener.

I really meant I wanted a dishwasher,
more money,
a bathrobe that fit him,
not so many parking tickets,
more kissing,
fancy bras.
"I wish we had romance and adventure," I said.
He unwrapped the L.A. Times and looked at the headlines.
He took a sip of coffee.
"That's not the way marriage is," he said. "That's not
the way real marriage is."

Posing for a Photograph

Which is my good side?
I try to remember the rules,
twist my body sideways.
Torque it's called.
I've heard it's better
to place the camera overhead,
shooting down.
Awkward yes.
But it minimizes shadows,
erases wrinkles.
Tongue pressed on roof of mouth,
behind the teeth
makes a perfect smile.
Not the clown grotesque,
nor the wimpy apologetic feint.
This is what I've heard at least.
Lick the lips for shine,
hiss like a snake.
Smile with your eyes.
Don't look right at the lens.
Look at the left ear.
Don't blink.

Life is like pulling a long rope.
After a while both ends look the same.
I choose only the pictures
that look nothing like me, burn
the ones
that show anything real.

Love Season

Life is
the slenderest of ladies,
blonde of course,
preferable.
Buddha's Smile tomatoes are ripe
for a short season.
Life grins her grins,
chores her chores,
skins a knee,
fights a fight
stronging as a bear.

Let me square your circle
she said,
while she rubbed my temple,
at which she also worshipped.
Later, she ate a ripe Heirloom,
the inners juicing,
splatters dripping
for a forensic scientist
on her white shirt.

May love be long and leave a mark,
a black line made with fine tip pen
on paper's creamy surface.
May the ink roll and puddle
its black juice,
from one side to everywhere.

In that deepest season,
she looked at me like June,
kissed me deep as winter snow,
sprouted a breath of sun.
She dared the wind
during this high season,
and made my hills
cover over with green.

Eating Beauty

"A child knows the world
by putting it part by part
into her mouth."
— JACK GILBERT

It should have lasted.
Her soul was nailed to her at birth.
A fierce explorer of the summer crusades,
she wobbled about the yard, a drunken bee,
intoxicated with learning.

Fragrance filled her open pores.
A wet Narcissis was plucked,
smelled dry and carried
home on a handkerchief,
a beloved warrior.

Trap doors for milk and mail
held secret notes,
a bent nail, a coin.
Once she found an earring,
set with green and red stones.

It was not a yard.
It was not a lawn.
It was not a garden.
It was something beyond.
It was a banquet of beauty.

But seasons change.
The moon scurried away.
Shadows spread over paradise,
and it rained
on a girl's
hummingbird heart.

What Luck

Somebody ran out on somebody.
Someone drank too much.
Over there, an unkind word.
In that kitchen, a knife drawer opens
or a bruise blooms on a neck.
At the shore, a freak wave is forming.

But tonight,
in the blue TV glow,
our dog lies between us.
The fire that could have started
in the old wires, didn't.
The errant cells
didn't color outside their lines.
Tonight, that peculiar wave
didn't crest in our direction.
Tonight my toes touch your toes
as we watch cars crash together
on the nine o'clock news.

Going the Distance

Not the unblemished hands but the work gloves.
Not the tasting menu but the ice cream truck.
Not the sermon preached but a whisper at dawn.
Not the sea but the serpent under a dress.
Not the diamond ring but a forty-seven-dollar band.
Not the gown of lace but a white cotton dress.
Not the resort honeymoon but two dented pillows.
Not the wedding silver but a scratched spoon.
Not the bridal gift but a nightly homecoming.
Not the philosophy of love but the spark and ignition.
Not the expert advice but endurance.
Not the compass but the long route from me to you.

About the Poet

SUZANNE O'CONNELL

grew up in Santa Monica. She now lives in Los Angeles near a spice and flavoring plant. Her neighborhood smells vanilla, cumin, or Worchestershire sauce, depending on demand.

She earned her MSW degree in social work from UCLA. Once the temperature and water level became just right, she became a poet.

She is grateful for her natural ability to parallel park, fold a fitted sheet, and make soup.

She is also grateful for her husband and friends and to own one inch of land in Alaska.

JEFFREY O'CONNELL

earned an MFA from UCLA. He has taught studio art classes starting in 1975 and continuing through 2015, principally at Santa Monica College and at Otis College of Art and Design.

He has exhibited in the Los Angeles area since 1972.

He was born in New York and moved to Los Angeles in 1961.

ACKNOWLEDGMENTS

Grateful acknowledgment is made to the editors of the following publications in which many of the poems in this collection have appeared.

North American Review
Poet Lore
Juked
Chiron Review
Red Savina Review
Edison Literary Review
Alembic
Glint Literary Journal
poeticdiversity
Poetry Super Highway
Writer's Resist
Diverse Voices Quarterly
Pennsylvania English
The Cape Rock
Bluestem Magazine
Evening Street Press
Rubbertop Review
Poetry Super Highway
Temenos
Green Hills Literary Lantern
San Diego Poetry Annual

Menacing Hedge
Carbon Culture Review
Existere
American Chordata
Door Is A Jar
Vainglory Press
Hiram Poetry Review
Westview
Storyscape Journal
After The Pause
Inscape
Drunk Monkeys
Gemini Magazine
Straight Forward Poetry
The Paragon Journal
Stirring
Steam Ticket
Paperplates
The Dallas Review
Alexandria Quarterly
Slab

Editor's note: a poem in this collection – *Crying is Expected in a Therapy Office* – earned Honorable Mention in the **2018 Steve Kowit Poetry Prize** and appeared for the first time in the *San Diego Poetry Annual 2018-19*. This marked the second time SUZANNE O'CONNELL earned honors in **The Kowit.**

CREDITS

Cover:

FRONT: *Sidewalk Face*
BACK: *After the Rain*
       images by JEFFREY O'CONNELL

POET: *Suzanne O'Connell*
       photograph by BAZ HERE

Interior:

SECTION AND PAGE ART –
       images by JEFFREY O'CONNELL

POET –
       photograph by ALEXIS RHONE FANCHER

ARTIST –
       self-portrait by JEFFREY O'CONNELL